The Spider of Lights
La Araña de Luces

Illustrated idioms in Spanish and English
Modismos ilustrados en español e inglés

Please note that the use of a particular idiom may vary within and across cultures and countries. This book does not portray the rich diversity of ways that idioms are interpreted and the important nuances of meaning that they can express.

El lenguaje varía, tanto entre culturas como en una misma cultura. No era nuestro objetivo mostrar la rica diversidad de interpretaciones de los modismos ni las matices de significado que puedan expresar.

Support for the production of this book was provided by McDaniel College's Faculty Development Committee and funding from the Charles A. Boehlke, Jr. Engaged Faculty Fellows Award.

Published by Lauren Dundes.
Illustrations by Patrick.

For permission or ordering requests, please contact: Ldundes@mcdaniel.edu

Book design by the Virtual Paintbrush.

ISBN 978-1-7370447-0-3 (hardcover)
ISBN 978-1-7370447-1-0 (paperback)
ISBN 978-1-7370447-2-7 (ebook)

LL UP YOUR SLEEVES
birse Las mangas

T'S PUT ON OUR BOOTS
ngámonos Las botas

YOU CAN'T TEACH AN OLD DOG NEW TRICKS
Perro viejo no aprende trucos nuevos

AN OLD PARROT CAN'T LEARN TO SPEAK
EL Loro viejo no aprende a hablar

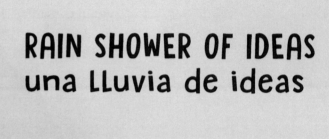

RAIN SHOWER OF IDEAS
una lluvia de ideas

BRAINSTORM
tormenta de cerebro

COPY CAT
gato de imitación

MONKEY OF IMITATION
mono de imitación

WHEN FROGS GROW HAIR
cuando Las ranas críen
pelo

TO HAVE A HEAD
FULL OF BIRDS
Tener La cabeza
LLena de pájaros

AN OLD DOG
Un perro viejo

BUILDING A HOUSE STARTING WITH THE ROOF
Empezar La casa por el tejado

GO FLY A KITE
Vete a volar
una cometa

DISCOVER THE CAKE
Descubrir el pastel

LET THE CAT OUT OF THE BAG
Liberar el gato de la bolsa

TO GO FROM BAD TO WORSE
Ir de mal en peor

TO JUMP FROM THE FRYING PAN INTO THE FIRE
Saltar del sartén al fuego

TO LEAVE GUATEMALA (GUATE-BAD) AND ENTER GUATEPEOR (GUATE-WORSE)
Salir de Guatemala y entrar en Guatepeor

YOU SNOOZE. YOU LOSE
Si una persona no está alerta en algo importante.
no sabe aprovechar la oportunidad y la pierde

THE SHRIMP THAT FALLS ASLEEP GETS
CARRIED AWAY BY THE CURRENT
Camarón que se duerme, se lo llev
la corriente

O RUN AWAY LIKE A BAT OUT OF HADES

orrer como un murciélago saliendo
el infierno

O LEAVE, SPILLING MILK

alir echando leches

THOSE WHO PERSEVERE REACH THEIR GOALS
El que persevera, alcanza

LIKE THE BURRO THAT PLAYED THE FLUTE
Como el burro que tocó la flauta

TOO LITTLE TO BE NOTICED
Tan poco que no lo nota nadie

A DROP IN THE BUCKET
Nada más una gota en el cubo

LIKE REMOVING A HAIR FROM A CAT
Como quitarle un pelo a un gato

CHANDELIER / SPIDER OF LIGHTS
Araña de Luces

THE END
Colorín, colorado
este libro se ha acabado

Lightning Source UK Ltd.
Milton Keynes UK
UKRC010909140621
385273UK00001BA/3

9 781737 044703